CRAYOLA COLOROLOGY™

COLOR IN SCIENCE, NATURE, ART, AND CULTURE

Mari Schuh

Lerner Publications ◆ Minneapolis

TABLE OF CONTENTS

COLORS ALL AROUND

Colors do amazing things!

Have you ever thought about how colors work? Scientists study how our eyes see color. They also study what happens when we mix colors.

Color is everywhere in nature. See the red on a ladybug's wings or the bright green skin on a tree frog. Find the golden sun in the bright blue sky.

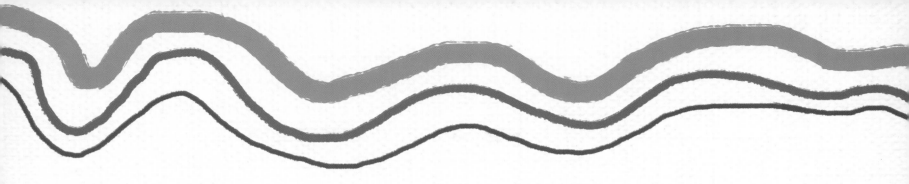

Color is important in art. Artists use color to create feelings in their artwork. They choose colors that work together.

Colors can have many meanings in culture. Colors stand for countries or holidays. People wear colors to express feelings, ideas, and places.

What do you notice about color? What are colors doing in your world?

CHAPTER 1
THE SCIENCE OF COLOR

We see colors all around us.

Color is everywhere!

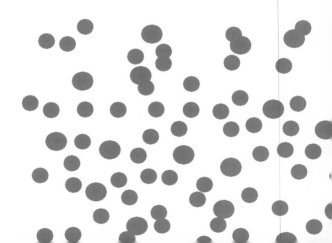

WHAT IS COLOR?

We see color because of light.

Light lets us see all the colors of a rainbow.

Sunlight shines through raindrops to make a rainbow.

Green, blue, yellow, and red. Everything we see has a color!

Light bounces off materials so we can see them.

Green light bounces off a green shirt.
Yellow light bounces off a yellow shirt.

Our eyes have tiny parts called cones.

Cones help us see colors.

Light touches the cones.

The cones tell our brains what colors we see.

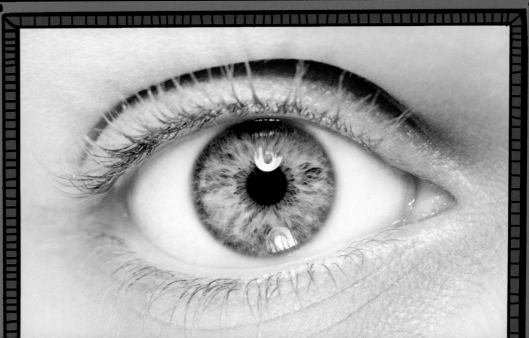

13

COLORS TOGETHER

Colors work together!

Some colors mix to make other colors.

Some colors help other colors stand out.

Yellow, red, and blue are called primary colors.

Primary colors can't be made from other colors.

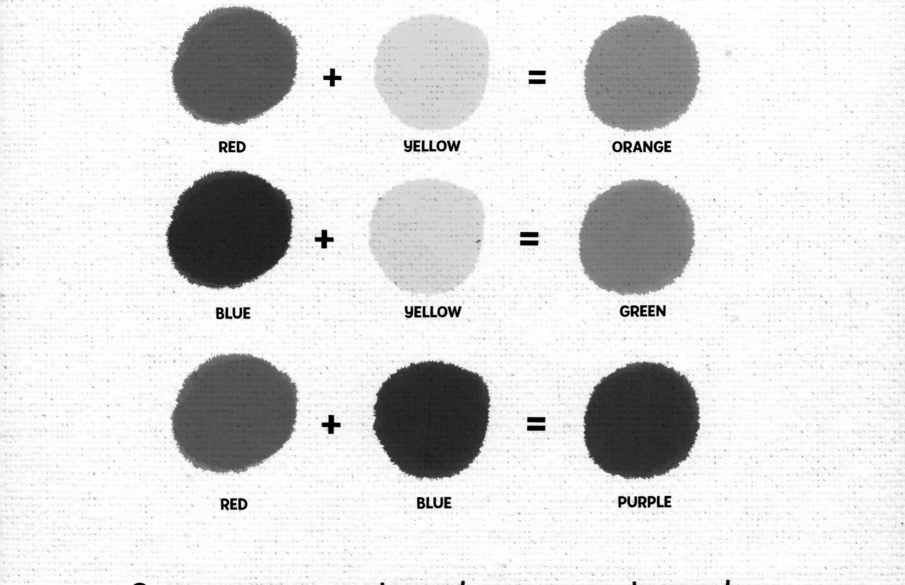

RED + YELLOW = ORANGE

BLUE + YELLOW = GREEN

RED + BLUE = PURPLE

Orange, green, and purple are secondary colors.

They are made by mixing two primary colors.

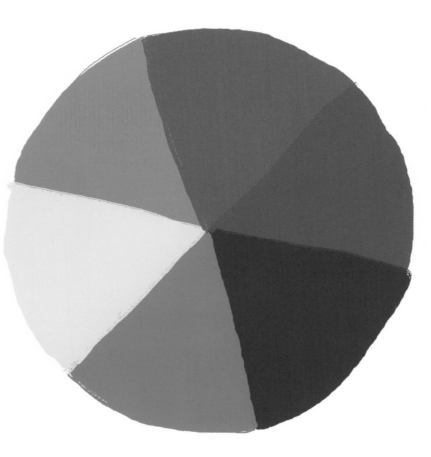

A color wheel shows us how colors are related.

Complementary colors are opposites on the color wheel.

Purple and yellow are complementary colors.
They are bold and easy to see!

Red, orange, and yellow are warm colors.

They remind us of the sun.

Blue, green, and purple are cool colors.

They remind us of water and the sky.

COLORS IN THE WORLD

We learn more about color all the time!

Scientists made a new bright blue pigment—by accident!

They called it YInMn blue for the chemicals it is made of.

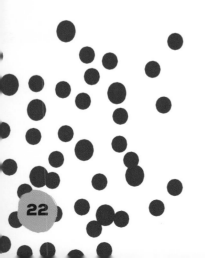

Colors look different with different colors around them.

Which red box looks the brightest?

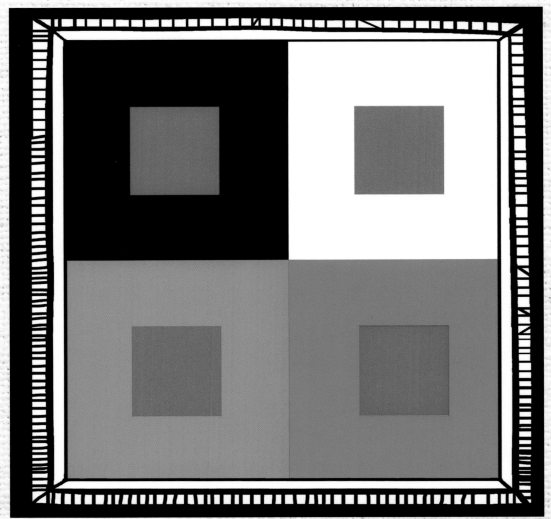

25

Sometimes colors stand out.

Sometimes colors blend in.

Can you find the insect hiding in the fall leaves?

Colors can make us feel calm.

They can also give us energy!

What colors do you like best?

CHAPTER 2
COLOR IN NATURE

High in the sky and deep in the ocean, nature is full of color!

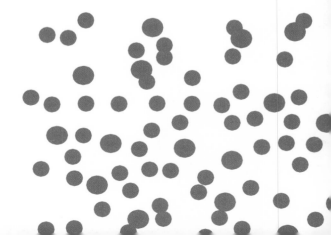

COLORS THAT HIDE

Do you see the lizards hiding in the hot desert?

They find rocks that match their skin color.

Many animals use color to hide from other animals.

33

A snowy owl hunts for food on the cold, snowy land. Its fluffy white feathers match the pure white snow.

Can you find the sneaky snake hiding in the rain forest?

A wild lion roams a grassland looking for food. The lion's tan fur helps it hide in the tall tan grass.

A butterfly rests on tree bark. The butterfly's dull colors blend in. Predators won't see it!

Dull colors help female birds hide. Hiding keeps the birds' eggs and young safe.

Which bird do you think is the female?

COLORS THAT WARN

The ladybug doesn't taste good to predators. Its red body warns birds and bugs to stay away.

A wasp's yellow body scares away predators. The wasp can sting!

Bright blue rings cover an octopus. Stay back!

The octopus has poison when it bites.

A skunk's black-and-white fur is easy to see. The colors warn others to stay far away.

The skunk can spray a stinky liquid!

Watch out!

A tree frog flashes its bright red eyes. The bright color surprises predators.

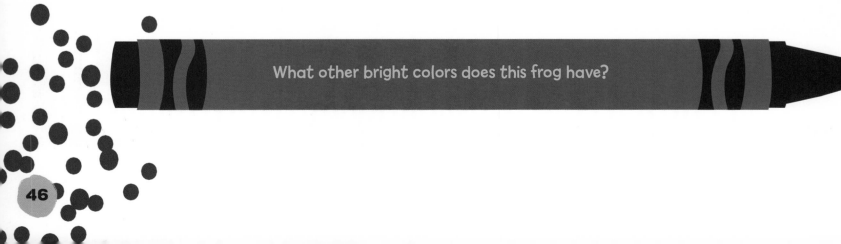

What other bright colors does this frog have?

COLORS THAT ATTRACT

Birds visit bright pink, yellow, and blue flowers.

The birds sip nectar from the flowers.

Look at these bold colors!

Male birds use their colorful feathers to get attention from females.

Big feathers and bright colors tell females that the males are healthy.

AMAZING COLORS

Amazing colors fill the night sky.
So many beautiful colors are found in nature.

What colors do you see outside?

CHAPTER 3

THE ART OF COLOR

Bright red, pale blue, and grassy green.

Art is bursting with color!

Artists use color to tell stories.

The colors they use make us feel different emotions.

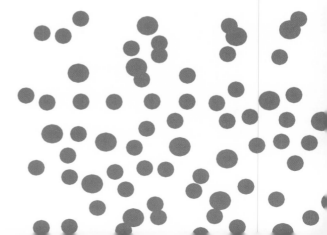

COLOR AND FEELING

Yellow,

orange,

and gold.

These bright, warm colors can make us feel happy.

Sunflowers, Vincent van Gogh, 1888

This painting uses many soft colors.

Green is cool and calm.

The Japanese Footbridge, Claude Monet, 1899

The woman's dress is beautiful shades of gold.

Why do you think her dress is gold?

Portrait of Adele Bloch-Bauer I, Gustav Klimt, 1907

61

LIGHT AND SHADOWS

Light colors stand out against dark colors.

What's the first thing you see in this painting?

Girl with a Pearl Earring, Johannes Vermeer, 1665

63

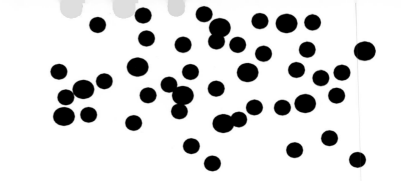

A day in the park was made with tiny dots of paint. Some places are sunny. Some places are shady.

Artists use dark colors to create shadows.

A Sunday on La Grande Jatte, Georges Seurat, 1884

See the shades of yellow and blue.

How many yellows and blues can you find?

The Boating Party, Mary Cassatt, 1893–1894

67

BOLD AND BRIGHT

Look at all the bold, bright colors!

Count all the colors you see.

Flight of an Aeroplane, Olga Vladimirovna Rozanova, 1916

69

Sometimes artists make paintings using only a few colors.

Artistic Architectonics, Lyubov Sergeevna Popova, 1916

71

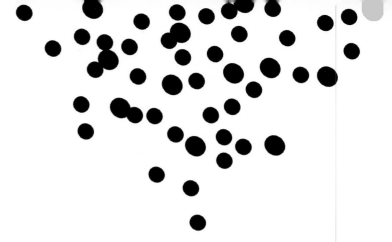

The reds, whites, and blues make your eyes move around this picture.

What else is made of red, white, and blue?

The 1920's . . . The Migrants Arrive and Cast Their Ballots,
Jacob Lawrence, 1974

COLORS OF THE OUTDOORS

See the big green leaves.

Where might this woman be?

How can you tell?

Self Portrait with Monkey, Frida Kahlo, 1938

75

Look at the colors in the sky and in the waves.

The colors make a dark storm.

What else can colors tell you?

The Great Wave off Kanagawa, Katsushika Hokusai, about 1831

CHAPTER 4
COLOR IN CULTURE

Color is part of culture. Colors have different meanings around the world.

Culture is the art we make, the clothes we wear, and the way we live.

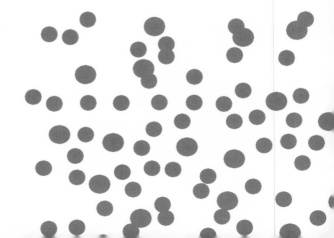

WE WEAR COLORS!

We wear colors every day.

You might wear team or school colors.

Or you can wear your favorite color.

How do you choose the colors you wear?

Some colors and styles of clothing remind us of countries and cultures.

Colored bracelets are popular in India.
These colorful hats come from Morocco.

People wear different colors around the world.

Colors can help us remember a country's history.

In Mexico, green is the color of freedom.

This woman in Peru wears a colorful shawl. What colors do you see?

CELEBRATING WITH COLOR

Colors help us celebrate.

People celebrate Holi in India, Nepal, and many other countries.

Holi is the festival of colors.

In spring, many people decorate Easter eggs.

Brightly colored eggs remind us of nature and new life.

Red is used to celebrate the Chinese New Year.

Red means good luck.

A COLORFUL WORLD

Countries have colors too.

Greece's flag is blue and white.

Blue is the color of the sea and sky.

White is the color of clouds.

We use colors to decorate our homes.

These colorful cloth plates come from Ethiopia.

THE MEANING OF COLOR

In India, blue is a very special color. It is the color of a god named Krishna.

People all around the world celebrate Day of the Dead with many colors. On this day, purple shows sadness, and white means hope.

Colorful skulls decorate Day of the Dead.

Weddings are a special time. People use many colors to celebrate.

Red is a popular color in Chinese and Indian weddings. Red stands for happiness, love, and beauty.

Colors are full of meaning. They help us celebrate, and they decorate our world.

What do colors mean to you?

MANY COLORS

Colors are all around the world.

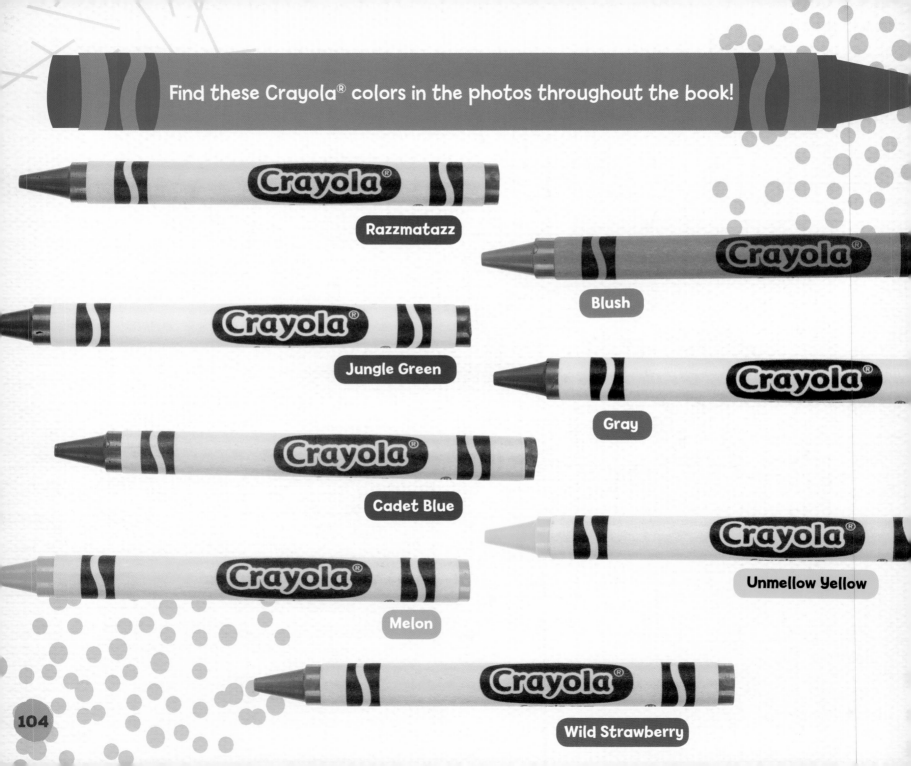

Find these Crayola® colors in the photos throughout the book!

Razzmatazz

Blush

Jungle Green

Gray

Cadet Blue

Unmellow Yellow

Melon

Wild Strawberry

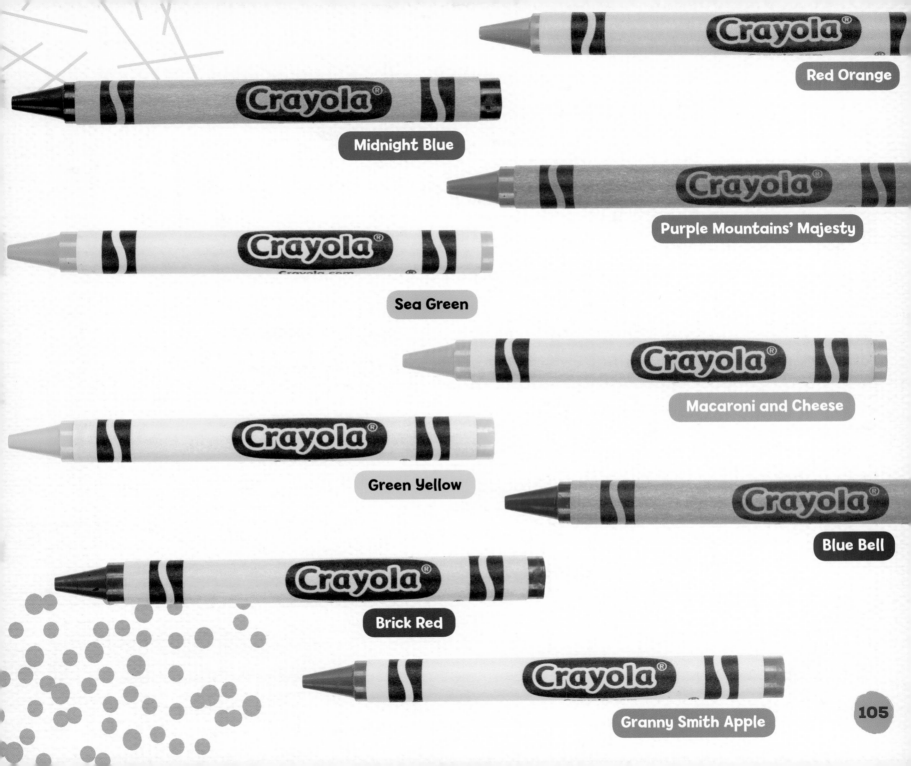

Red Orange

Midnight Blue

Purple Mountains' Majesty

Sea Green

Macaroni and Cheese

Green Yellow

Blue Bell

Brick Red

Granny Smith Apple

GLOSSARY

artists: people who make art, such as paintings, sculptures, and music

bold: able to stand out very clearly

calm: peaceful

Chinese New Year: an important Chinese holiday on the first day of the year on the Chinese calendar

color wheel: a diagram that shows how colors are related

complementary colors: colors that are very different from each other. Complementary colors are opposites on the color wheel.

cones: special cells in the eye that sense colored light

culture: the laws, ideas, way of life, and traditions of a group of people

Day of the Dead: a holiday mostly in Mexico to celebrate life and family

desert: a dry area with little rain and few plants

emotions: strong feelings. Happiness, sadness, and anger are emotions.

grassland: a large, open area covered with grass

history: past events

Holi: a holiday to celebrate spring

holy: having to do with worship, religion, or a higher being

mural: a painting on a wall or building

nature: the world of living things and the outdoors. Plants and animals are part of nature.

nectar: a sweet liquid found in many flowers

pale: having a light color

poison: a substance that can harm or kill

predators: animals that hunt other animals for food

primary colors: colors that can't be made from other colors. Red, yellow, and blue are primary colors.

rain forest: a thick forest where a lot of rain falls

secondary colors: colors that are made by mixing two primary colors. Orange, green, and purple are secondary colors.

shades: the degrees of lightness or darkness of a color

shadows: shaded areas made when light is blocked

symbols: things that stand for something else

TO LEARN MORE

BOOKS

Adamson, Heather. *Purple.* Minneapolis: Bullfrong Books, 2014.
    Learn about purple plants, animals, and rocks and how colors work in nature.

Blevins, Wiley. *Colors All Around.* South Egremont, MA: Red Chair, 2016.
    Read this book about a young girl discovering all the colors around her.

Borth, Teddy. *Yellow Animals.* Minneapolis: Abdo, 2015.
    Read about yellow animals throughout the world and how their color helps them.

O'Connell, Emma. *We Love Green!* New York: Gareth Stevens, 2016.
    Read about green things, from turtles and snakes to grapes and leaves.

Osburn, Mary Rose. *I Know Colors.* New York: Gareth Stevens, 2017.
    Explore color by reading about common objects you might see every day.

Shepherd, Jodie. *Crayola Spring Colors.* Minneapolis: Lerner Publications, 2018.
    Explore the wide variety of colors found during the spring season.

WEBSITES

Animal Coloring Pages
    http://www.crayola.com/free-coloring-pages/plants-and-animals/animals-coloring-pages/
    Visit this website to color several animal coloring pages.

Colors around the World
    https://visual.ly/community/infographic/other/colors-around-world
    Visit this website to learn what different colors mean around the world.

The Color Wheel
http://www.kidzone.ws/science/colorwheel.htm
Learn about the color wheel.

Crayons with Paint
http://www.crayola.com/things-to-do/how-to-landing/crayons-with-paint/
Visit this website to learn how to make some of your own art using crayons and paint.

Explore Color
http://www.crayola.com/explore-colors/
Learn all about color as you work on coloring pages and color experiments.

Explore the Outdoors
http://pbskids.org/outdoors/
Explore the great outdoors and all the colors found in nature.

Light and Color
http://pbskids.org/dragonflytv/show/lightandcolor.html
Learn more about light and color.

Melting Marker Colors
http://www.crayola.com/crafts/melting-marker-colors-craft/
Explore more with color, and create your own art using markers and water.

Tree Coloring Pages
http://www.coloring.ws/trees.htm
Visit this website to work on several tree coloring pages.

What Colors Mean
https://www.factmonster.com/features/speaking-language/what-colors-mean
This website explains the many meanings of color.

INDEX

PHOTO ACKNOWLEDGMENTS

The images in this book are used with the permission of: kirillov alexey/Shutterstock (linen background throughout); © Lisa F. Young/Dreamstime, p. 7 (left); © Ashifa R./Dreamstime, p. 7 (top right); © Alain Lacroix/Dreamstime, p. 7 (bottom right); GODONG/Science Source, pp. 9, 102 (bottom left); © Michael Flippo/Dreamstime, p. 11; iStock/Freder, p. 13 (top); iStock/stock_colors, p. 13 (bottom); iStock/konradlew, p. 15 (top left); iStock/Syldavia, p. 15 (top right); iStock/nevodka, p. 15 (bottom left); iStock/CathyKeifer, p. 15 (bottom right); iStock/SumikoPhoto, p. 15 (center); Rosenfeld Images Ltd/Science Source, p. 16; Action Plus Sports Images/Alamy, p. 19; © maxime raynal/flickr (CC BY 2.0), p. 20; © Christian Araujo/Dreamstime, p. 21; Mas Subramanian/Wikimedia Commons (CC BY-SA 4.0), p. 23; Thomas Marent/Minden Pictures/Getty Images, pp. 27, 102 (top right); iStock/YuriyS, p. 29 (top); iStock/SolStock, p. 29 (bottom); Natapong Supalertsophon/Getty Images, p. 31 (top left); Jorg Greuel/Getty Images, p. 31 (top right); iStock/Grafner, p. 31 (bottom left); Josemaria Toscano/Shutterstock, pp. 31 (bottom right), 102 (bottom right); iStock/KS-Art, p. 31 (center); iStock/Dopeyden, p. 33 (top); iStock/Photon-Photos, p. 33 (bottom); UIG Premium/Getty Images, p. 34; iStock/FotoSpeedy, p. 35; Kjersti Joergensen/Shutterstock, p. 36; iStock/numismarty, p. 37; iStock/mirceax, p. 39; iStock/eli_asenova, p. 41 (top); Adam Gault/Getty Images, p. 41 (bottom); iStock/Subaqueosshutterbug, p. 43; Thomas Kitchin & Victoria Hurst/Getty Images, p. 45; © Hotshotsworldwide/Dreamstime, p. 47; Adventure_Photo/Getty Images, p. 49 (top); Tongho58/Getty Images, p. 49 (bottom); Allan Baxter/Getty Images, p. 51 (top); Darshan Khanna Photography/Getty Images, p. 51 (bottom); Vincent Demers Photography/Getty Images, p. 53; iStockom/kosmos111, p. 55; The National Gallery, London/Wikimedia Commons (CC 1.0 PDM), p. 57; Gift of Victoria Nebeker Coberly, in memory of her son John W. Mudd, and Walter H. and Leonore Annenberg, Image courtesy of the Board of Trustees, National Gallery of Art, Washington DC, p. 59; GalleriX/Wikimedia Commons (CC 1.0 PDM), pp. 61, 103 (bottom left); Mauritshuis/Wikimedia Commons (CC 1.0 PDM), p. 63; Art Institute of Chicago/Wikimedia Commons (CC 1.0 PDM), pp. 65, 103 (top left); Chester Dale Collection, Image courtesy of the Board of Trustees, National Gallery of Art, Washington DC, p. 67; © Art Museum, Samara, Russia/Bridgeman Images, p. 69; © Private Collection/Bridgeman Images, p. 71; © 2017 The Jacob and Gwendolyn Knight Lawrence Foundation, Seattle/Artists Rights Society (ARS), New York, image via © San Diego Museum of Art, USA; Gift of Lorillard, a Division of Loews Theatres, Inc./Bridgeman Images, p. 73; © 2017 Banco de México Diego Rivera Frida Kahlo Museums Trust, Mexico, D.F./Artists Rights Society (ARS), New York, image via © Albright-Knox Art Gallery/Art Resource, NY, p. 75; © Private Collection/Bridgeman Images, p. 77; © Nila Newsom/Dreamstime, pp. 79 (top), 102 (top left); © Sebikus/Dreamstime, p. 79 (bottom); Crystal Kirk/Shutterstock, p. 81 (top left); © Kameel4u/Dreamstime, p. 81 (top right); iStock/ERphotographer, p. 81 (bottom left); © Monkey Business Images/Dreamstime, p. 81 (bottom right); © Nagarjun Kandukuru/flickr (CC BY 2.0), p. 81 (center); © Maciej Czekajewski/Dreamstime, p. 83 (left); © Nikhil Gangavane/Dreamstime, p. 83 (right); CHRISTIAN DE ARAUJO/Shutterstock, p. 85 (top); Bartosz Hadyniak/Getty Images, p. 85 (bottom); Poras Chaudhary/Getty Images, p. 87 (top); iStock/Intellistudies, p. 87 (bottom); © Redbaron/Dreamstime, p. 89; View Stock/Getty Images, p. 91 (bottom); P_Wei/Getty Images, p. 91 (top); Samot/Shutterstock, p. 93; iStock/mtcurado, p. 95; Shyamalamuralinath/Shutterstock, p. 97 (top); iStock/agustavop, p. 97 (bottom); iStock/goodesign10, p. 99 (top left); shuige/Getty Images, p. 99 (bottom left); IVY PHOTOS/Shutterstock, p. 99 (right); iStock/huePhotography, p. 101; © Harun/Dreamstime.com, p. 103 (top right); Nicolas Ayer/EyeEm/Getty Images, p. 103 (bottom right).

Cover (l-r): © Nila Newsom/Dreamstime; SantiPhotoSS/Shutterstock; © Museum of Modern Art, New York, USA/Bridgeman Images; © Nikhil Gangavane/Dreamstime.

Official Licensed Product
Lerner Publications Company
A division of Lerner Publishing Group, Inc.
241 First Avenue North
Minneapolis, MN 55401 USA

For reading levels and more information, look up this title at www.lernerbooks.com.

Main body text set in Billy Infant Regular 24/30.
Typeface provided by SparkyType.

Library of Congress Cataloging-in-Publication Data

Names: Schuh, Mari C., 1975- author.
Title: Crayola colorology : color in science, nature, art, and culture / Mari Schuh.
Other titles: Colorology | Color in science, nature, art, and culture
Description: Minneapolis : Lerner Publications, [2018] | Audience: Ages 4–8. | Audience: K to grade 3. | Includes
    bibliographical references and index.
Identifiers: LCCN 2017048244 (print) | LCCN 2017053378 (ebook) | ISBN 9781541529144 (eb pdf) |
    ISBN 9781541528796 (pb : alk. paper)
Subjects: LCSH: Color—Juvenile literature. | Crayons—Juvenile literature.
Classification: LCC QC495.5 (ebook) | LCC QC495.5 .S36864 2018 (print) | DDC 535.6—dc23

LC record available at https://lccn.loc.gov/2017048244

Manufactured in the United States of America
1-44726-35556-11/14/2017